BONE BROTH BREAKTHROUGH

Dr. Josh Axe

NOTICE TO READER

This book is not intended to provide medical advice or to take the place of medical advice and treatment from your personal physician. Readers are advised to consult their doctors or qualified health professionals regarding specific health questions. Neither the publisher nor the author takes responsibility for possible health consequences of any person reading or following the information in this book. All readers, especially those taking prescription or over-the-counter medications, should consult their physicians before beginning any nutrition or supplement program.

† These statements have not been evaluated by the Food and Drug Administration. This product is not intended to diagnose, treat, cure or prevent any disease.

Visit our website at www.BoneBrothProtein.com.

ISBN-13: 978-0-692-67657-8

Cover photography and design: Allison Brochey

Printed in the USA

CONTENTS

ABOUT

DR. JOSH AXE

Dr. Josh Axe, DNM, DC, CNS, is a doctor of natural medicine, doctor of chiropractic and clinical nutritionist with a passion to help people get well using food as medicine and operates one of the worlds largest natural health websites: www.DrAxe.com.

He is the author of the groundbreaking health book *Eat Dirt*, which uncovers the hidden causes and cures of leaky gut syndrome. Dr. Axe is an expert in digestive health, functional medicine, natural remedies and dietary strategies for healing. He has been featured on many television shows, including the Dr. Oz Show, CBS and NBC, and has his own *Eat Dirt* program running on select PBS TV stations.

Dr. Axe founded one of the largest functional medicine clinics in the world, in Nashville, TN, and has been a physician for many professional athletes.

DrAxe.com is one of the most visited websites worldwide for healthy recipes, herbal remedies, nutrition and fitness advice, essential oils, and natural supplements.

CHAPTER 1

BONE BROTH IS NOT HYPE: IT'S A BIG HELP

Considered to be one of the most ancient and remarkable nutritional substances on the planet, bone broth is a beneficial "elixir" made from simmered animal bones. Not only does bone broth taste great and provide numerous nutrients and beneficial compounds, it's also versatile and easy to use in many recipes.

Yet the vast majority of the general public passes up the opportunity to boost its health with bone broth, often unaware of how incredibly good it is for you. Instead, if any broth is consumed, it's often the store-bought, processed, sodium-filled, nutritionally bankrupt versions.

Bone broth is a great place to find valuable amino acids, collagen, gelatin and trace minerals. In fact, there are dozens of different nutrients found within bone broth, many of which can't be obtained easily from other commonly eaten foods.

BOOST YOUR BODY WITH BONE BROTH'S NUTRITION

Bone broth could be called "nature's multivitamin." How so? It's packed with:

- Over 19 easy-to-absorb, essential and non-essential amino acids (the building blocks of proteins)
- Collagen/gelatin, which helps form connective tissue
- Nutrients that support digestive functions, immunity and brain health†

Did you get that? It literally boosts every part of your body, from your gut to your brain, from your muscles to your ligaments.

It's also relatively low in calories, yet very high in minerals and other chemical compounds that many people lack. There's no doubt that bone broth makes a great everyday addition to your diet.

THE TOP 6
BONE BROTH NUTRIENTS

1. GLYCOSAMINOGLYCANS

Glycosaminoglycans (GAGs) have the primary role of maintaining and supporting collagen and elastin that take up the spaces between bones and various fibers. GAGs are supportive for digestive health since they help restore the intestinal lining, which is why a deficiency in these nutrients has been linked to digestive challenges.†[1]

Several important GAGs are found in bone broth, including glucosamine, hyaluronic acid and chondroitin sulfate.

2. GLUCOSAMINE

There are two main types of naturally occurring glucosamine: hydrochloride and sulfate. Both help keep up the integrity of cartilage, which is the rubbery substance within joints that acts like a natural cushion. Studies show that glucosamine can become depleted as we get older, so supplements are often used to support joint health.†

An easy and relatively inexpensive way to obtain glucosamine naturally is from drinking more bone broth, which helps support cartilage health, acting as an alternative to pricey glucosamine supplements.[2] Consuming more glucosamine can help support joint health, flexibility and comfort.†

3. HYALURONIC ACID

Found throughout connective, epithelial (skin) and neural tissues, hyaluronic acid contributes to cell proliferation, differentiation and mitigation, allowing our cells to perform various functions throughout the body as needed. It offers support for multiple skin types and promotes healthy aging, cell rejuvenation and skin firmness.†[3]

4. CHONDROITIN SULFATE

Chondroitin sulfate is a beneficial glycosaminoglycan found in the cartilage within the joints of all animals. It's often used to support joint health and comfort, especially in combination with glucosamine.

Studies have found that supplementing with chondroitin supports healthy inflammation response as well as cardiovascular health, bone health, skin health and healthy cholesterol levels.†[4]

5. MINERALS AND ELECTROLYTES

Bone broth provides essential minerals, including electrolytes, all delivered in an easy-to-absorb form. Electrolytes found within bone broth include calcium, magnesium and potassium (not to mention many other minerals, such as phosphorus), which are important for supporting healthy circulation, bone density, nerve-signaling functions, heart health and digestive health. When added sodium levels are kept low, bone broth contains an ideal balance of sodium and potassium to support cellular health and efficiency.†

6. COLLAGEN

Collagen is the main structural protein found within the human body that helps form connective tissue and "seals" the protective lining of the gastrointestinal tract. It's also the gel-like, smooth structure that covers and holds our bones together, allowing us to glide and move freely.

Irritation within the gut impairs normal digestive functions and causes permeability, allowing particles to pass into the bloodstream, known as leaky gut.†

As a rich source of gelatin, bone broth protects and seals the mucosal lining of the GI tract, which means it improves nutrient absorption and also helps keep particles from leaching out where they shouldn't be.

As a complex protein, collagen contains a whopping 19 amino acids, with a mix of both non-essential (also called conditional) and essential types. Many of the amino acids found within collagen must be obtained from our diets since our bodies cannot make them on their own.†

AMINO ACIDS IN COLLAGEN

Here are the key amino acids found in collagen:

PROLINE

- Proline, which is the chief component of collagen, is essential for building integrity for healthy skin, hair and nails. †
- It is also essential for building the gut lining and facilitating digestive function, yet most people are lacking this amino acid in their diets because they don't consume organ meats or bone broth on a regular basis. †
- Proline is needed for tissue repair within the joints and arteries. In addition, it helps support healthy blood pressure levels. †
- As a key component of collagen found within joints, proline buffers our bodies from the effects of vibration or shock and helps us hold on to valuable cartilage as we get older. †[5]
- This amiono acid also supports healthy cardiovascular function. †

GLUTAMINE

- Glutamine supports the body in the maintenance of healthy muscle tissue during and after periods of exercise, and it helps with muscular fatigue. †
- Research shows that glutamine supports digestive health, healthy immune system response and energy levels. †[6]
- It also provides "fuel" to our cells and supports a healthy intestinal lining. †
- It supports synthesis of glutathione, one of the body's most powerful antioxidants. †

GLYCINE

- Approximately one-third of the protein found in collagen is glycine.†
- One of glycine's most important roles is helping to form muscle tissue by converting glucose into usable energy that feeds muscle cells.†
- This amino acid is found in high quantities in muscles, the skin and various tissues.†
- Research shows glycine has important roles in digestion and central nervous system function.†[7]
- Glycine promotes detoxification and cleansing.†

ARGININE

- Arginine breaks down into nitric oxide within the body, which is an important compound for arterial and cardiovascular health.†[8]
- Nitric oxide allows for better vasodilation, meaning the widening of arteries and relaxation of muscle cells and blood vessels that allows for better circulation.†
- Arginine also helps the body make more protein from other amino acids, which is important for repairing muscle tissue, promoting normal wound healing, sparing tissue wasting, boosting the metabolism and aiding in proper growth and development.†

CHAPTER 2

BONE BROTH & COLLAGEN BY THE NUMBERS

Bone broth is very versatile and can be made using bones from just about any type of animal. The bones are usually simmered for about 24-48 hours, often mixed with other nutrient-dense foods, such as vegetables, herbs and spices, and uses an acidic liquid like apple cider vinegar to liberate key minerals.

Many people prefer one type of bone broth over another. But you can simply use bones from any animal you have left over after cooking and then remove the meat. You can also buy bones from a farmer's market, a local health food store, a butcher or even online.

Some of the most popular types of bones to use come from cows, veal, lamb, bison, venison, chicken, duck, goose, turkey or fish.

BEEF BONE BROTH

- Beef broth is one of the richest, most savory and nutrient-packed bone broths and is high in type 1 and type 3 collagen (see next page).
- Often it's made using veggies, herbs and spices, including garlic, celery, carrots, onions and even apple cider.
- It's high in bone marrow and amino acids, especially when you include some larger bones that contain a high amount of cartilage and collagen.

CHICKEN AND TURKEY BONE BROTH

- You've likely had chicken soup or broth many times in your life, but the homemade version is far superior to any canned variety.
- Many homemade chicken broths are made using chicken feet, knuckles, skin, giblets or other organ parts, which are high in healthy fatty acids and type 2 collagen.

FISH BONE BROTH

- Fish bone broth has been used in Asia for thousands of years.
- The broth made from fish tends to be milder and lighter, since the bones are smaller.
- Fish stock is a great addition to soups, stews and noodle dishes.
- It's a great source of iodine, calcium, amino acids and healthy fats (especially when you use wild-caught fish).
- This broth is a good alternative to chicken or beef stocks if you don't eat meat or have easier access to whole fish.

Meanwhile, there are at least 16 types of collagen within the human body, but 80 to 90 percent of the collagen consists of types 1, 2 and 3.[9]

TYPE 1

- The most abundant and strongest type of collagen within the human body is type 1.
- It's made of eosinophilic fibers and found in tendons, ligaments, bone, the dermis (skin) and various organs.
- Type 1 collagen is used to form bones and support wound healing since it's extra strong and capable of being stretched without tearing.†

TYPE 2

- Cartilage within our joints is mainly composed of type 2 collagen, the primary protein found in our connective tissues.
- Researchers at Harvard's Beth Israel Deaconess Medical Center in Boston found that supplementing with type 2 collagen supports healthy inflammation response.†[10]
- Other studies have found that people who supplement their diets with type 2 collagen show significant enhancements in daily activities and a general improvement in their quality of life.†[11]
- Type 2 collagen is primarily found in chicken and turkey broth and is also the best for repairing and sealing the gut lining.†
- If you want to support digestive and immune system health, make sure you get type 2 collagen in your daily diet.†

TYPE 3

- Type 3 collagen is a major component of the extracellular matrix that makes up our organs and skin.
- It helps give skin its elasticity and firmness, plus forms our blood vessels and tissue within the heart.†

CHAPTER 3

6 REASONS TO CONSUME BONE BROTH EVERY DAY

In one way or another, just about every culture throughout history has used a form of bone broth to improve health and support a healthy immune system. In ancient China, for example, gelatin was prized as a natural way to maintain muscle strength, bone density and ease of movement into older age, since it protects joints, bones and muscle tissue from damage.†[12]

Our ancestors valued bone broth as a "nose-to-tail" approach to using all parts of an animal, including the bone marrow and skin that are often discarded today. Using these parts was an inexpensive, convenient way to obtain an abundance of minerals, proteins and other nutrients while also flavoring recipes and avoiding waste.

According to a report in the *New York Times*, many years ago people made bone broth by dropping fire-heated rocks into the stomachs of whatever animals they managed to kill. Years later, with the invention of stoves and pots, bone broth became easier than ever to make and turned into a "staple in virtually every corner of the culinary world."[13]

Although animal ligaments, joints and bones might not seem very appealing to eat, they are highly nutritious parts of the animal that hold ingredients not readily available in muscle meat or plant foods. Throughout history, bone broth was sipped on not only because it was comforting, but also because it was said to help calm the nerves, improve energy and promote healthy aging.†

Up until recently, Western culture has mostly ignored the benefits of traditional bone broths. Many people are hesitant to consume animal parts other than meat or to cook with bones, marrow and cartilage. Luckily, today more emphasis is being placed on the importance of obtaining nutrients naturally, rather than turning to synthetic supplements. Bone broth is making a huge comeback and is even being called a "superfood."

Over the past century, more and more research has shown us that overall health highly depends on the state of the microbiome, or the mix of microorganisms living within our intestinal tract. Most systems, if not every system, of the body are interrelated to the health of our gut, which is dependent on the state of our microbiome. That's because an unbalanced ratio of bad-to-good bacteria, fungus, yeast and microbes living within the gut alters how the immune system works.†

In fact, a very large percentage of our immune system activity — about 70 to 80 percent — actually resides in the digestive tract, which holds trillions of bacteria and other microbes that affect nearly every bodily function in one way or another.

Because it's chock-full of nutrients and easy to digest (even for people with compromised gut health), bone broth plays a major role in many programs designed to help support digestive functions and nutrient absorption, as well as to restore integrity of the gut lining. This includes the GAPS Diet, the Maker's Diet, the Bone Broth Diet and other cleansing, fasting or immune support programs.†

6 BENEFITS OF BONE BROTH

By regularly drinking bone broth or using it in recipes, you help promote healthy gut integrity while reducing permeability and inflammation. Here are the six major benefits of bone broth.†

1. PROTECTS JOINTS†

Bone broth is one of world's best sources of natural collagen, the protein found in animals — in their bones, skin, cartilage, ligaments, tendons and bone marrow. As we get older, our joints naturally experience wear-and-tear, and we become less flexible.

Why does that matter? As we age, cartilage diminishes as it gets attacked by antibodies (age-related degradation of joint cartilage). As bone broth simmers, collagen from the animal parts leaches into the broth and becomes readily absorbable to help restore cartilage.

One of the most valuable components of bone broth is the protein gelatin, which acts like a soft cushion between bones that helps them "glide" without friction. Gelatin also provides us with building blocks that are needed to form and maintain strong bones, helping take pressure off of aging joints and supporting healthy bone mineral density.†

Research done by the Department of Nutrition and Sports Nutrition for Athletics at Penn State University found that when athletes supplemented with collagen over the course of

24 weeks, the majority showed significant improvements in joint comfort and a decrease in factors that negatively impacted athletic performance.†[14]

2. BENEFITS THE GUT†

Studies show that gelatin is beneficial for restoring strength of the gut lining and fighting food sensitivities (such as to wheat or dairy), helping with the growth of probiotics ("good bacteria") in the gut and supporting healthy inflammation levels in the digestive tract. A report published in the *Journal of Clinical Gastroenterology* found that gelatin effectively supports intestinal health and integrity.†[15]

Bone broth is easily digested and soothing to the digestive system, unlike many other foods that can be difficult to fully break down. After all, a food is really only useful if we have the means of absorbing its nutrients.

Studies have found that in individuals with digestive imbalances, serum concentrations of collagen are decreased.[16] Because the amino acids in collagen build the tissue that lines the colon and entire GI tract, supplementing with collagen can support healthy digestive function.†

3. MAINTAINS HEALTHY SKIN†

Collagen helps form elastin and other compounds within skin that are responsible for maintaining skin's youthful tone, texture and appearance. Collagen integrity is accredited with helping reduce the visible signs of wrinkles, decreasing puffiness and fighting various other signs of aging. Many people report a decrease in cellulite when consuming foods and supplements containing collagen. Why? Because cellulite forms due to a lack of connective tissue, causing skin to lose its firm tone.†

Double-blind, placebo-controlled studies investigating the age-defending properties of collagen found that 2.5-5 grams of collagen hydrolysate (CH) used among women aged 35-55 once daily for eight weeks supported skin elasticity, skin moisture, transepidermal water loss (dryness) and skin roughness.

At the end of only four weeks, those using collagen showed a statistically significant improvement in comparison to those using a placebo with regard to skin moisture and skin evaporation, plus noticeable decreases in signs of accelerated aging, all with little to no side effects.†[17]

4. SUPPORTS IMMUNE SYSTEM FUNCTION†

One of the best things about bone broth is its gut supportive benefits, which as described previously have a holistic effect on the body and support healthy immune system function.†

Leaky gut occurs when undigested particles from foods seep through tiny openings in the weakened intestinal lining and enter the bloodstream, where the immune system detects them and becomes hyperactive. This increases inflammation and leads to dysfunctions all over, as the immune system releases high levels of antibodies that cause an autoimmune-like response and attacks healthy tissue.†

Bone broth is one of the most beneficial foods to consume to restore gut health and, therefore, support immune system function and healthy inflammation response. Collagen/gelatin and the amino acids proline, glutamine and arginine help seal these openings in the gut lining and support gut integrity.

Traditionally made bone broths are believed to support healthy inflammatory response and normal immune system function. [18]

Bone broth can even promote healthy sleep, boost energy during the day and support a healthy mood.†

5. BOOSTS DETOXIFICATION†

Today in the Western world, the average person is exposed to an array of environmental toxins, pesticides, artificial ingredients and chemicals of all sorts. While the human body has its own means of detoxifying itself from heavy metals and other toxic exposures, it often has a hard time keeping up when flooded with an overwhelming amount of chemicals.

Bone broth is considered a powerful detoxification agent since it helps the digestive system expel waste and promotes the liver's ability to remove toxins, helps maintain tissue integrity and improves the body's use of antioxidants. † Bone broth also contains potassium and glycine, which support both cellular and liver detoxification.†

Some of the ways in which bone broth boosts detoxification is by supplying sulfur (especially when you add veggies, garlic and herbs to your broth) and glutathione, which is a phase 2 detoxification agent that lowers oxidative stress.

Stanford University's Medicine Preventative Research Center found that glutathione helps with elimination of fat-soluble compounds, especially heavy metals like mercury and lead. It also boosts the absorption of various nutrients, the use of antioxidants and liver-cleansing functions.†[19]

Bone broth also increases intake of essential minerals, which act like chelators to remove toxins by stopping heavy metals from attaching to mineral receptor sites.

6. AIDS THE METABOLISM AND PROMOTES ANABOLISM†

Bone broth is a great way to obtain more glutathione, which studies show plays important roles in antioxidant defense, nutrient metabolism and regulation of cellular events. A 2004 study published in the *Journal of Nutrition* stated that glutathione's roles and benefits include regulating gene expressions, DNA and protein synthesis, cell proliferation and apoptosis, signal transduction, cytokine production and immune responses.†[20]

Amino acids found in bone broth have numerous metabolic roles, including building and repairing muscle tissue, supporting bone mineral density, boosting nutrient absorption and synthesis, and maintaining muscle and connective tissue health.

Glycine found within collagen helps form muscle tissue by converting glucose into usable energy, plus it slows cartilage, tissue and muscle loss associated with aging by improving the body's use of antioxidants. Studies have revealed that glycine protects skeletal muscle loss and stops the expression of genes associated with age-related muscle protein breakdown.†[21]

Glutamine is another amino acid that's important for a healthy metabolism, since it helps us maintain energy by sending nutrients, including nitrogen, to our cells. Arginine also has the role of breaking down nitric oxide that helps improve circulation and sends blood and nutrients to cells throughout the body, improving muscle and tissue integrity and promoting normal wound healing.†

CHAPTER 4

HOW TO MAKE A GREAT BONE BROTH

There are a few important basics to consider when making a great bone broth. First, while animal components and water alone can make a simple and healthy broth, combining it all with some select vegetables, herbs and spices appears to have a synergistic effect, working together to be more beneficial than either alone.

Speed-wise, it's easy to simply use the animal carcass and bones, but for additional collagen and gelatin benefits, consider using parts including chicken feet and neck. No matter what animal you decide to base your bone broth on, however, from chicken to cow to lamb to fish, make sure that it's as free of chemicals as possible.

The essential ingredients of a solid bone broth, according to bestselling author Sally Fallon, co-founder of the Weston A. Price Foundation, are bones, fat, meat, vegetables and water.

If you're making beef broth or lamb broth, you should brown the meat before putting it into a stock pot. Fish and poultry, meanwhile, are fine to put in a pot without browning first. Then you simply add a bit of apple cider vinegar to your pot to help draw the minerals from the bones.

For added nutrients and flavor, I suggest using sea salt, carrots, onions and celery along with parsley (or even better, Herbes de Provence). To receive additional multisystemic benefits, add ginger, turmeric and other tasty powerful herbs.

As you can see, the options abound for bone broth. You can use different animals as the base, make simple or more complex versions, choose different flavoring ingredients or even choose the convenient option of a ready-to-mix bone broth protein powder.

IF YOU DO DECIDE TO MAKE BONE BROTH AT HOME, HERE ARE THE STEPS TO TAKE:

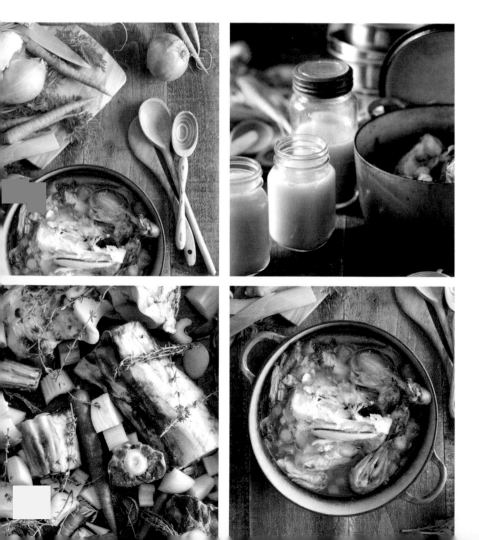

1 Choose a large pot for the stovetop or a crockpot. Place the bones into the pot or crockpot and cover with water. (If you're making beef or lamb broth, you should brown the meat before putting it into a stock pot. Fish and poultry, including chicken feet and the neck, are fine to put in a pot without browning first.) Make sure you leave plenty of room for water to boil.

2 Add two tablespoons of apple cider vinegar to the water prior to cooking. This helps pull out important nutrients from the bones.

3 Heat slowly, bringing it to a boil and then reducing the heat to a simmer for at least six hours. Skim off the fat on top as it arises.

4 Now, while six hours is the minimum time to extract those valuable nutrients from the bones, chicken bones can cook for 24 hours and beef bones can cook for 48 hours. (Fish stock, using the bones and the head, requires the least amount of time, and sometimes 1–2 hours is adequate.) Overall, a low temperature and long cooking time are necessary in order to first preserve and then fully extract the nutrients in and around the bones.

5 You can also add in vegetables, such as onions, garlic, carrots and celery, for added nutrient value. For standard flavor, add herbs and spices, such as parsley or Herbes de Provence. For an additional kick (and more health benefits), consider adding ginger and turmeric.

6 Remove from the heat and let it cool slightly. Discard solids and strain the remainder in a bowl through a colander.

7 Let the broth cool to room temperature, cover and chill. Use within a week or freeze for up to three months.

CHAPTER 5

BONE BROTH PROTEIN POWDER

What if I told you there was an easy way to receive all of the benefits of bone broth without having to spend hours making it or paying a high price for the frozen variety? That's where Bone Broth Protein™† powder comes in. Bone Broth Protein is bone broth liquid that is dehydrated, making it into a concentrated source of high-quality and tasty powder.

This is THE protein powder I recommend to all of my patients because of the incredible health benefits, plus its convenience and ease of use. As wonderful as bone broth is, preparing and consuming it regularly is a daunting task to say the least. With Bone Broth Protein, one can consume health-giving bone broth in literally seconds with no prep or cleanup at home, work or when traveling.

A quality Bone Broth Protein (not to be confused with bouillon cubes, which are packed with artificial flavorings and sodium) comes with the same benefits of a homemade broth, but it's also just as tolerable for digestion and versatile in so many recipes. In addition, Bone Broth Protein supplies 20 grams of muscle-building protein to support healthy muscle building and maintenance and metabolism.†

THE CONVERSION IS SIMPLE

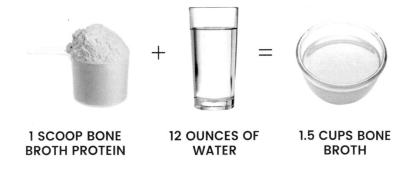

| 1 SCOOP BONE BROTH PROTEIN | 12 OUNCES OF WATER | 1.5 CUPS BONE BROTH |

† These statements have not been evaluated by the Food and Drug Administration. This product is not intended to diagnose, treat, cure or prevent any disease.

What is the difference between Bone Broth Protein and collagen powder? Most collagen powders on the market today contain types 1 and 3 collagen but don't have the other beneficial nutrients found in chicken bone broth.

Bone Broth Protein contains high levels of type 2 collagen but also contains vital minerals, including potassium, magnesium, calcium, selenium, glycosaminoglycans (GAGs), hyaluronic acid, glucosamine and chondroitin.

Because Bone Broth Protein contains higher levels of type 2 collagen (support for the gut, skin, immune system and joints) while bovine collagen contains higher levels of types 1 and 3 collagen (support for hair, skin, bones and muscle), I recommend my patients use both on a daily basis.†

5 BIG BENEFITS OF BONE BROTH PROTEIN†

1 **Saves You Time** — Bone Broth Protein is easier than making bone broth yourself at home, not as messy and will give back time to your already busy schedule.

2 **Super Cost-Effective** — If you go out and purchase a container or jar of bone broth liquid from a retailer or your local farmers market, you will pay an average of $5.50 per serving versus paying only $2.25 per serving of Bone Broth Protein. You save twice as much!

3 **Packed with Protein** — With 20 grams of high-quality, easily digestible protein per serving, Bone Broth Protein is a fantastic way to help you and your family meet your daily protein requirements.†

4 **Superior Protein** — Many people find that protein powders can be difficult to digest. For those with dairy or egg sensitivities, whey, casein and egg white protein can cause digestive and other issues, as can brown rice and pea protein for those who don't digest grains or legumes well.†

5 **Diet and Gut-Friendly** — If you're following a gut-supportive diet, leaky gut diet, elimination diet, gluten-free diet, low-carbohydrate diet or a real food diet, this is the perfect protein powder for you. Bone Broth Protein is high in proline and glutamine, which are amino acids that support the digestive system.†

---

8 GREAT WAYS TO USE BONE BROTH PROTEIN

SMOOTHIES

Add one scoop of Bone Broth Protein (vanilla or chocolate) to your smoothie every morning for an added 20 grams of gut-friendly protein.†

FOOD BARS AND PROTEIN SNACKS

Make your own homemade protein bars that are great snacks for the whole family and a way to stay healthy while traveling.†

CROCKPOT AND SOUP RECIPES

Use Pure or Turmeric Bone Broth Protein as a direct replacement for bone broth and additionally season with sea salt, parsley and garlic.

ANCIENT GRAINS

Use with quinoa, rice and oats to create a super-grain with a balanced amino acid profile of 20 grams of body-building protein per serving.†

HEALTHY DESSERTS

Want to support your metabolism and add protein to your dessert? Add protein and gut-friendly nutrients to desserts, such as high-protein cookies and protein puddings.†

NATURAL HEALTH SUPPLEMENT

Use Bone Broth Protein as a supplement for healthy joints, skin, hair, gut health and immune support.†

WORKOUT MEALS

Mix Bone Broth Protein directly in water or with dairy, almond or cashew milk plus fruit for pre-workout and post-workout snacks to aid recovery, metabolism and muscle support.†

BONE BROTH CLEANSE

Mix Bone Broth Protein in daily smoothies and juices for an effective full-body cleanse (due to its high levels of glycine and potassium). See the next chapter for a transformational cleansing program.†

CHAPTER 6

BONE BROTH BODY CHALLENGE

To maximize the benefits of bone broth — gently detoxifying the body while supporting your gut health, lean muscle, metabolism, skin health, immune system support and even your joints — I strongly recommend that you begin consuming bone broth daily in one form, one way or another. †

The easiest, most healthful and fun way to do this? Take my Bone Broth Body Challenge! There are four unique plans for you to choose from, and you'll be amazed how it will help transform not only your gut health, but your entire body. †

BONE BROTH BODY CHALLENGE!
FOUR PLANS. CHOOSE YOURS.

3-DAY BONE BROTH BURST

- Daily, consume 4-6 servings of bone broth* exclusively for three days — each serving should be either 12 ounces of homemade bone broth or one scoop of Bone Broth Protein (Pure and/or Turmeric variety) mixed in 12 ounces of water, sipped slowly.
- If you encounter additional thirst, drink only unsweetened herbal infusions, tea or water.

3-DAY BONE BROTH CLEANSE

- Consume one serving of bone broth or Bone Broth Protein for breakfast.
- Consume a bone broth smoothie for lunch and dinner.
- When thirsty, consume only unsweetened herbal infusions, tea or water.

7-DAY BONE BROTH CHALLENGE**

- Prepare and consume three recipes per day.
- Choose from breakfast/smoothies, snacks or main dishes.
- When thirsty, consume only unsweetened herbal infusions, tea or water.

30-DAY BONE BROTH TRANSFORMATION**

- 8 a.m. breakfast: consume either a Bone Broth Protein smoothie, one serving of bone broth or Bone Broth Protein mixed in water.
- 12 p.m. lunch: consume either a bone broth main dish or a bone broth snack bar.
- 6 p.m. dinner: consume a bone broth main dish.
- Dessert: have two bone broth desserts each week.

Note: All readers, especially those taking prescription or over-the-counter medications, should consult their physicians before beginning any nutrition or supplement program.

*Remember, 1.5 cups of homemade bone broth is the nutritional equivalent of one scoop of Bone Broth Protein mixed in 12 ounces of water.

**If hungry, consume more bone broth or Bone Broth Protein servings throughout the day.

3-DAY BONE BROTH CLEANSE

DAY 1

Breakfast
12 ounces bone broth or one serving of Bone Broth Protein (Pure or Turmeric) mixed in water or almond milk

Lunch
Bone Broth Blueberry Protein Shake (see recipe on page 57)

Dinner
Mocha Fudge Smoothie (see recipe on page 65)

DAY 2

Breakfast
12 ounces bone broth or one serving of Bone Broth Protein (Pure or Turmeric) mixed in water or almond milk

Lunch
Green Detox Smoothie (see recipe on page 65)

Dinner
Pumpkin Pie Smoothie (see recipe on page 58)

DAY 3

Breakfast
12 ounces bone broth or one serving of Bone Broth Protein (Pure or Turmeric) mixed in water or almond milk

Lunch
Strawberry Coconut Smoothie (see recipe on page 70)

Dinner
Carrot Ginger Smoothie (see recipe on page 60)

7-DAY BONE BROTH CHALLENGE

	MONDAY	TUESDAY	WEDNESDAY
BREAKFAST	Strawberry Coconut Smoothie	12 ounces bone broth*	12 ounces bone broth* mixed with almond milk
LUNCH	Butternut Bisque	Tuna Salad	Bison Cabbage Broth
DINNER	Egg Drop Soup	Avgolemono	Broccoli Cauliflower Soup

3 MEALS PER DAY

8 A.M. BREAKFAST
bone broth smoothie
or one serving of pure
Bone Broth Protein

12 P.M. LUNCH
bone broth snack/bar
or bone broth main
dish

6 P.M. DINNER
bone broth
main dish

THURSDAY	FRIDAY	SATURDAY	SUNDAY
Bone Broth Blueberry Protein Shake	12 ounces bone broth*	Mocha Fudge Smoothie	Gut-Repair Shake
Quinoa-Stuffed Peppers	Indian Curry Soup	Carrot Cake Bar	Chicken Salad
Gingered Beef & Broccoli Soup	Turkey & Rice Congee	Slow Cooker Scalloped Sweet Potatoes	"Noodle" Bowls

*Or one serving of Bone Broth Protein (Pure or Turmeric) mixed in 12 ounces water

30-DAY
BONE BROTH
TRANSFORMATION†

For best results, repeat this 14-day program twice and an additional two days for a total of 30 days

	DAY 1	DAY 2	DAY 3
8 AM	Bone Broth Blueberry Protein Shake	Pre-Workout Electrolyte Drink	Veggie Frittata
NOON	Chicken Salad	Almond Fig Bar	Bison Cabbage Broth
3 PM	12 ounces bone broth*	12 ounces bone broth*	Golden Tea
6 PM	Butternut Bisque	Avgolemono	Quinoa-Stuffed Peppers + Chocolate Chip Cookies

8 A.M. BREAKFAST
bone broth smoothie or breakfast recipe

12 P.M. LUNCH
bone broth main dish or bone broth snack bar

3 P.M. SNACK
12 ounces bone broth or one serving of pure Bone Broth Protein mixed in water

6 P.M. DINNER
bone broth main dish
Dessert: limit yourself to 2 bone broth desserts each week

DAY 4	DAY 5	DAY 6	DAY 7
Carrot Ginger Smoothie	Coconut Porridge	Protein Pancakes	Banana Nut Bread
Butternut Bisque	Egg Salad	Post-Workout Muscle-Building Shake	Blueberry Macadamia Bar
12 ounces bone broth*	12 ounces bone broth*	Golden Tea	12 ounces bone broth*
Indian Curry Soup	Meatball Soup	Turkey and Rice Congee + Raspberry Ice Cream	Creamy Tomato Soup

*Or one serving of Bone Broth Protein (Pure or Turmeric) mixed in 12 ounces water

30-DAY BONE BROTH TRANSFORMATION†

For best results, repeat this 14-day program twice and an additional two days for a total of 30 days

	DAY 8	DAY 9	DAY 10
8 AM	Green Detox Smoothie	High-Protein Raisin Oatmeal	Gut-Repair Shake
NOON	Creamy Tomato Soup	Gingered Beef & Broccoli Soup	Tuna Salad
3 PM	12 ounces bone broth*	Golden Tea	12 ounces bone broth*
6 PM	Slow Cooker Scalloped Sweet Potatoes	"Noodle" Bowls	Meatball Soup + Raspberry Smoothie

DAY 11	DAY 12	DAY 13	DAY 14
Bone Broth Coffee	Oatmeal Cookie Smoothie	Strawberry Coconut Smoothie	Chai Waffles
Carrot Cake Bar	Broccoli Cauliflower Soup	Tasty Turkey Burgers	Mushroom Miso Soup
12 ounces bone broth*	Golden Tea	12 ounces bone broth*	12 ounces bone broth*
Egg Drop Soup	Quinoa-Stuffed Peppers	Gingered Beef & Broccoli Soup + Frozen Chocolate Bananas	Beef & Butternut Squash Soup

*Or one serving of Bone Broth Protein (Pure or Turmeric) mixed in 12 ounces water

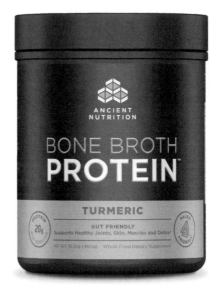

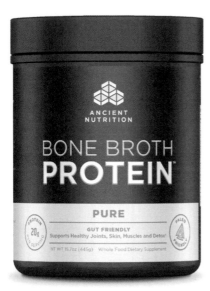

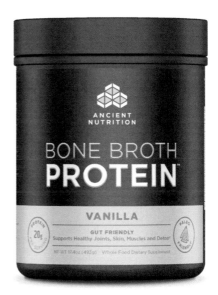

BONE BROTH PROTEIN POWDER

#1 GUT-FRIENDLY PROTEIN POWDER †

BONE BROTH PROTEIN™
PURE & TURMERIC

- 20g Protein | No Carbs | No Sugars
- Gut-Friendly | Paleo-Friendly | 100% Natural
- Dairy-Free | Soy-Free | Grain-Free | Nut-Free | Gluten-Free
- Amino Acids, Collagen Type 2, Glucosamine, Chondroitin, Hyaluronic Acid and Minerals
- Mix in Protein Shakes, Smoothies and Raw Juices. Use It in Your Favorite Recipe or Side, Such as Hummus, Quinoa or Food Bars
- Support Healthy Joints, Skin, Muscles and Detox †

ALSO AVAILABLE, NATURALLY DELICIOUS CHOCOLATE & VANILLA

- 20g Protein | Low Carbs (2g) | Low Sugars (1g)
- Mixes Easily in Water, Juice, Unsweetened or Sweetened Almond Milk, Coconut Milk or as Part of a Nutritious Protein Shake
- Add Flavored Bone Broth Protein to Create Protein-Packed Desserts, Pancakes and Snacks!

CHAPTER 7

BONE BROTH RECIPES

BREAKFASTS & SMOOTHIES

PRE-WORKOUT
ELECTROLYTE DRINK

BONE BROTH BLUEBERRY PROTEIN SHAKE

- 12 ounces coconut (full-fat) or almond milk
- 1 cup frozen blueberries
- ½ banana
- ¼ teaspoon cinnamon (optional)
- 1 scoop Bone Broth Protein (Vanilla or Chocolate)

1 Place all ingredients in blender and purée until smooth, adding additional nut milk and ice to blend as necessary.

PRE-WORKOUT ELECTROLYTE DRINK

- 12 ounces coconut water
- 1 cup frozen mango
- ½ cup pineapple chunks
- juice from ½ lime and ½ lemon
- ¼ – ½ inch fresh piece ginger
- 1 scoop Bone Broth Protein (Pure or Vanilla)

1 Place all ingredients in blender and purée until smooth, adding more coconut water to blend as necessary.

OATMEAL COOKIE SMOOTHIE

- ½ cup cooked gluten-free oats
- 8 raw cashews
- 12 ounces water
- 2 Medjool dates, pitted
- pinch of cinnamon
- pinch of sea salt
- 1 scoop Bone Broth Protein (Pure)

1 Place all ingredients in a blender and purée until smooth.

PUMPKIN PIE SMOOTHIE

- ½ cup pumpkin purée
- ½ cup cooked butternut squash
- ½ teaspoon pumpkin pie spice
- ½ teaspoon vanilla extract
- 12 ounces nut milk or water
- 1 scoop Bone Broth Protein (Pure)

1 Place all ingredients in a blender and purée until smooth, adding more liquid if needed.

PUMPKIN PIE
SMOOTHIE

CARROT GINGER SMOOTHIE

- 1 cup carrots, steamed
- ½ cup fennel, steamed
- ½ inch ginger root, sliced
- 12 ounces water
- 1 scoop Bone Broth Protein (Pure)

1 Place all ingredients in a blender and purée until smooth.

BONE BROTH CLEANSER DRINK

- 2 carrots, steamed
- 2 celery stalks, steamed
- 12 ounces water
- 1 cup chopped cilantro
- 1 scoop Bone Broth Protein (Turmeric)

1 After steaming veggies, place all ingredients in a blender with water. Purée until smooth.

PEACH PROBIOTIC SMOOTHIE

- ½ banana
- ¾ cup frozen peaches
- ½ cup coconut (full-fat) or goat milk kefir (or yogurt)
- 12 ounces nut milk
- ½ teaspoon pumpkin pie spice (or cinnamon)
- 1 scoop Bone Broth Protein (Pure or Vanilla)
- ⅛ teaspoon vanilla extract

1 Place all ingredients in a blender and purée until smooth, adding more liquid if needed.

PEACH PROBIOTIC
SMOOTHIE

MOCHA FUDGE
SMOOTHIE

64

MOCHA FUDGE SMOOTHIE

- 1 cup frozen banana
- ¼ cup raw cashews
- 2 tablespoons cocoa powder
- 1 teaspoon carob powder
- 1 teaspoon instant coffee or espresso powder
- 12 ounces coconut milk (full-fat)
- 1 teaspoon raw honey
- 1 scoop Bone Broth Protein (Pure)

1 Place all ingredients in a blender and purée until smooth, adding water and ice to blend as necessary.

GREEN DETOX SMOOTHIE†

- 1 pear
- 1 cup cucumber, peeled and chopped
- 12 ounces coconut water or water
- 1 teaspoon ginger root, minced
- 1 cup fresh spinach
- 1 scoop Bone Broth Protein (Pure or Turmeric)

1 Preheat the oven to 350 F. Line a baking sheet with parchment paper. Slice pear in half and place face down on a baking sheet. Cook for 20 minutes. Place all ingredients in a blender and purée until smooth. Add more liquid/ice if necessary.

PROTEIN PANCAKES

SERVES: 4–6   TIME: 20 MINUTES

- 1 cup applesauce
- 3–4 eggs
- ¼ cup coconut oil, melted
- ⅓ cup coconut flour
- 4 scoops Bone Broth Protein (Pure or Vanilla)
- ½ teaspoon Himalayan salt
- toppings: maple syrup, coconut nectar, or raw honey and cinnamon

1 In a medium bowl, whisk applesauce, eggs and oil together thoroughly. Stir in coconut flour, protein powder and Himalayan salt and allow to sit for 5 minutes.

2 In a large skillet over medium-low heat, melt additional coconut oil. Once hot, drop batter into skillet and fry until bubbles form on one side. Flip, finish cooking and enjoy breakfast.

3 Top with maple syrup, coconut nectar, or raw honey and cinnamon.

THIN MINT
SMOOTHIE

THIN MINT SMOOTHIE

- 12 ounces coconut milk (full-fat)
- 3 drops peppermint extract
- 3 tablespoons cocoa powder
- 1 scoop Bone Broth Protein (Chocolate)
- ½ cup of ice

1 Place all ingredients in a blender and purée until smooth. Add more liquid/ice if necessary.

GUT-REPAIR SHAKE†

- 1 pear
- 12 ounces coconut milk (full-fat)
- 1 teaspoon ginger root, minced
- 1 teaspoon raw honey
- 1 scoop Bone Broth Protein (Pure or Turmeric)

1 Preheat oven to 350 F.

2 Slice pear in half and place face down on a baking sheet. Cook for 20 minutes.

3 Place all ingredients in a blender and purée until smooth, adding water and ice to blend as necessary.

STRAWBERRY COCONUT SMOOTHIE

- 1 cup frozen strawberries
- 12 ounces coconut milk (full-fat)
- 1 tablespoon raw honey
- 1 teaspoon bee pollen
- 1 scoop Bone Broth Protein (Pure)

1 Place all ingredients in a blender and purée until smooth. Add more liquid/ice if necessary.

POST-WORKOUT MUSCLE BUILDING SHAKE†

- 3 tablespoons almond butter
- 12 ounces plain kefir
- ½ cup gluten-free oats
- 1 banana
- 1 scoop Bone Broth Protein (Pure or Vanilla)
- 3 raw eggs (optional)

1 Place all ingredients in a blender and purée until smooth, adding water and ice to blend as necessary.

STRAWBERRY COCONUT SMOOTHIE

HIGH-PROTEIN RAISIN OATMEAL

SERVES: 1–2   TIME: 20 MINUTES

- 1 cup gluten-free, steel-cut oats
- 1 scoop Bone Broth Protein (Pure) mixed with 12 ounces water (or 12 ounces bone broth)
- ½ cup Medjool dates, pitted and thinly sliced
- ¾ cup raw honey
- 2 tablespoons coconut oil, melted
- 1 teaspoon vanilla extract
- 2 teaspoons cinnamon
- ½ cup almond butter
- ½ cup raisins

1 Soak oats overnight in water.

2 Drain oats and add to a pot along with 12 ounces of water and protein powder. Heat over medium-high heat.

3 Bring mixture to a boil and then reduce heat and allow to simmer for 5 minutes.

4 In a food processor, add dates, honey, oil, vanilla, cinnamon and almond butter and pulse until combined.

5 Stir in raisins until well combined. Serve and enjoy!

COCONUT PORRIDGE

SERVES: 1–2   TIME: 15 MINUTES

- 1 cup coconut milk (full-fat)
- 1 scoop Bone Broth Protein (Pure or Vanilla)
- ½ cup coconut, shredded
- 1–2 tablespoons maple syrup
- 1 tablespoon hemp seeds
- 1 tablespoon chia seeds
- 1 tablespoon flaxseeds
- ¼ teaspoon vanilla extract
- ¼ teaspoon cinnamon
- ¼ teaspoon sea salt
- berries (optional)

1 In a medium pot over medium-high heat, place all ingredients and bring to a boil. Reduce heat and allow to simmer for 5 minutes.

2 Add porridge to a high-speed blender and blend until thick and creamy.

3 Optionally, top with berries.

VEGGIE OMELET

SERVES: 1   TIME: 10 MINUTES

- 1 garlic clove, minced
- ¼ cup each: chopped red pepper, green pepper and mushroom
- 2 tablespoons chopped red onion
- 2 tablespoons ghee
- 1 scoop Bone Broth Protein (Pure or Turmeric)
- 3 eggs
- ¼ cup raw goat cheese
- ½ teaspoon each: oregano, chives, black pepper and sea salt

1 In a saucepan over medium-low heat, sauté garlic, peppers, mushroom, onion and ghee.

2 In a small bowl, mix protein powder with eggs.

3 Add egg mixture to saucepan with veggies. Add cheese on top and allow to cook for 1 minute, then fold into an omelet.

4 Cook for 1 minute, and then flip and cook for another minute.

5 Remove from heat and top with oregano, chives, black pepper and sea salt. Enjoy!

GOLDEN TEA

SERVES: 2   TIME: 5 MINUTES

- 12 ounces nut milk
- ½ cup water
- 1 scoop Bone Broth Protein (Turmeric)
- 1 tablespoon ghee
- 1 tablespoon raw honey
- cinnamon or pumpkin spice to taste

1   In a small saucepan over medium-low heat, pour nut milk, water and turmeric protein powder. Warm for 2 minutes.

2   Add in ghee and honey and stir for another 2 minutes.

3   Stir again and pour into glasses. Add cinnamon or pumpkin spice to taste.

CHAI WAFFLES

SERVES: 2-3 SEVEN-INCH WAFFLES   TIME: 20 MINUTES

- ½ cup chickpea flour
- ¼ cup almond flour
- ¼ cup cassava flour
- 1 scoop Bone Broth Protein (Pure)
- ½ teaspoon baking powder
- ½ teaspoon each: cardamom, ginger and cinnamon
- ¼ teaspoon each: nutmeg and cloves
- ⅛ teaspoon sea salt
- 2 eggs
- ¼ cup applesauce
- ¼ cup water
- toppings: raw honey, grass-fed butter and fresh berries

1 Preheat a waffle maker according to manufacturer's instructions.

2 In a large mixing bowl, whisk flours, protein powder, baking powder, spices and sea salt.

3 In a separate bowl, whisk eggs, applesauce and water.

4 Add dry ingredients to wet ingredients and stir until well combined.

5 Scoop ⅓ cup onto waffle maker and cook 2-3 minutes.

6 Repeat for each waffle.

7 Top with raw honey, grass-fed butter and fresh berries.

BONE BROTH COFFEE

SERVES: 1–2   TIME: 5 MINUTES

- 12 ounces organic brewed coffee
- 1 tablespoon grass-fed butter
- 1 tablespoon coconut oil
- 1 scoop Bone Broth Protein (Pure, Vanilla or Chocolate)

1 Brew coffee to desired strength.

2 In a high speed blender, add in coffee, butter, coconut oil and protein powder.

3 Blend on high and serve in a large mug.

VEGGIE FRITTATA

SERVES: 4   TIME: 40 MINUTES

- 1 scoop Bone Broth Protein (Pure or Turmeric) mixed in 8 ounces water
- ½ teaspoon sea salt
- ½ red onion, diced
- 1 cup small broccoli florets
- 1 cup mushrooms, sliced
- ½ red pepper, diced
- 8 eggs
- 1 tablespoon fresh basil, minced
- ¼ teaspoon crushed red pepper or chipotle flakes (optional)

1 In a large, all-metal sauté pan over medium-high heat, bring bone broth and sea salt to a simmer. Add veggies and simmer for 8 minutes, uncovered. Reduce heat to low. Turn the oven on and set to low broil.

2 In a medium bowl, whisk eggs, basil and optional pepper flakes together thoroughly. Add egg mixture to pan and stir to combine.

3 Cover and cook on stovetop for 10-15 minutes. Broil, still covered, for 3-7 minutes, watching carefully, until eggs are set.

BANANA NUT BREAD

SERVES: 6−8   TIME: 55 MINUTES

- 4 eggs
- 3 medium overly ripe bananas, mashed
- ¼ cup raw honey
- ¼ cup coconut milk
- 1 tablespoon vanilla extract
- 2 teaspoons baking soda
- 2¼ cups almond flour
- ½ teaspoon sea salt
- ½ teaspoon cinnamon
- 1 scoop Bone Broth Protein (Pure)

1 Preheat the oven to 350 F. In a bowl, mix eggs, banana, honey, coconut milk and vanilla.

2 In a separate bowl, combine the remaining ingredients.

3 Combine both mixtures and stir until well incorporated.

4 Grease a bread pan and pour in batter. Bake for 35−50 minutes.

MAIN DISHES

BUTTERNUT BISQUE

SERVES: 4   TIME: 1 HOUR

- 4 tablespoons ghee
- 1 red onion, minced
- 1 Granny Smith apple, peeled, cored and chopped
- 2 teaspoons dried sage
- 1 butternut squash, peeled, seeded and cut into chunks
- 3 scoops Bone Broth Protein (Pure) mixed with 36 ounces of water (or 36 ounces bone broth)
- 1 teaspoon nutmeg
- sea salt and pepper, to taste

1 In a large pot over medium heat, melt ghee. Add onion, apple and sage, stirring occasionally, for about 8 minutes.

2 Add squash and bone broth. Bring to a simmer and cook until squash is fork tender, about 15-20 minutes.

3 Using an immersion blender, purée until smooth (be careful blending hot liquids).

4 Heat through and season with nutmeg, sea salt and pepper before serving.

QUINOA-STUFFED PEPPERS

SERVES: 2–4   TIME: 45 MINUTES

- 1 scoop Bone Broth Protein (Pure) mixed with 16 ounces water (or 16 ounces bone broth)
- 1 cup quinoa, rinsed and drained
- sea salt and pepper, to taste
- 2 bell peppers, halved and seeded
- 1 teaspoon olive oil plus additional for drizzling
- 1 onion, chopped
- 1 zucchini, chopped
- 2 tablespoons garlic, minced
- 1 tablespoon dried Italian seasoning
- ½ cup fresh parsley, chopped

1 Preheat the oven to 450 degrees F.

2 In a medium saucepan over medium-high heat, combine bone broth and quinoa. Bring to a boil. Reduce heat to low, cover and cook for 15 minutes. Remove from heat and let stand, covered, for 5 minutes. Fluff with a fork and set aside.

3 Meanwhile, sprinkle bell peppers with sea salt and pepper. Place on a baking sheet and roast cut side down until skin begins to char, about 20 minutes. Remove from the oven and reduce oven temperature to 375 degrees F.

4 While bell peppers roast, heat oil in a skillet over medium heat. Add onion, zucchini, garlic and Italian seasoning. Season with salt and pepper. Cook, stirring occasionally, until vegetables are tender, 10–12 minutes. Add reserved quinoa. Sprinkle with parsley and stir to combine.

5 Turn bell peppers cut side up and fill halves evenly with quinoa mixture. Drizzle with oil as desired. Heat in the oven until warmed through.

TURKEY AND RICE CONGEE

SERVES: 4–6   TIME: 1.5 HOURS

- 3 scoops Bone Broth Protein (Turmeric) mixed in 36 ounces water (or 4 cups chicken or turkey bone broth)
- 1 cup brown rice
- 1 tablespoon fresh grated ginger root
- 1 teaspoon sea salt
- 3 carrots, peeled and sliced
- 1 large red onion, diced
- 1 bunch kale, washed, torn into pieces, stems discarded or saved for juicing
- 2 garlic cloves, pressed or minced
- 2 cups shredded turkey

1 In a large pot over medium heat, bring bone broth and rice to a simmer. Add ginger. Reduce heat to medium low and cook, partially covered, for 45 minutes.

2 Add sea salt, carrots, onion, kale, garlic and turkey to soup and simmer, partly covered, for 25 minutes.

3 Remove from heat, stir and serve.

BISON CABBAGE BROTH

SERVES: 8–10   TIME: 45 MINUTES

- 2 tablespoons coconut oil
- 1½ pounds ground bison
- 2 onions, diced
- 3 scoops Bone Broth Protein (Pure) mixed in 36 ounces water (or 4 cups beef bone broth)
- 2 bay leaves
- 1 cabbage, chopped thinly
- 12 carrots, peeled and sliced
- 5 potatoes, diced
- sea salt and pepper, to taste

1 In a large pot over medium-high heat, melt coconut oil and add ground bison. Stir until partly cooked through. Add onions and finish cooking bison.

2 Add remaining ingredients and cover. Stir occasionally, reducing to medium heat once it simmers. Cook for 30 minutes and serve.

MEATBALL SOUP

SERVES: 4–6   TIME: 50 MINUTES

- 1¹/₂ pounds ground bison or beef
- 2 eggs, whisked
- ¹/₂ teaspoon + 1 teaspoon sea salt, divided
- 1 teaspoon smoked paprika or cayenne
- 2 tablespoons coconut oil
- 3 scoops Bone Broth Protein (Pure) mixed with 36 ounces water (or 36 ounces bone broth)
- 1 teaspoon sea salt
- 2 bay leaves
- 4 carrots, peeled and chopped
- 1 large sweet potato, chopped
- 1 cup green beans
- 1 cup green peas
- 2 tomatoes, chopped

1 Mix meat, eggs, ¹/₂ teaspoon sea salt and paprika or cayenne together. Roll into small meatballs.

2 In a large pot over medium heat, heat oil. Add meatballs and cook for 5–8 minutes, or until brown.

3 Add bone broth, 1 teaspoon sea salt, bay leaves, carrots and sweet potato, bringing to a simmer over medium-high heat.

4 Add remaining ingredients and simmer for 20 minutes, or until sweet potato is ready to be eaten.

INDIAN CURRY SOUP

SERVES: 4   TIME: 35 MINUTES

- 4 scoops Bone Broth Protein (Turmeric) mixed in 48 ounces water (or 6 cups chicken bone broth)
- 1 tablespoon fresh grated ginger root
- 2-3 tablespoons Indian curry powder
- 1 yellow onion, chopped
- 2 cups small cauliflower florets
- 2 red peppers, chopped
- 1 teaspoon cayenne pepper (optional)
- 1 can (14 ounces) coconut milk (full-fat)

1 In a large pot over medium heat, bring bone broth and ginger to a simmer. Add curry powder, onion, cauliflower, peppers and cayenne.

2 Bring to a boil, then reduce heat to medium-low and simmer for 15 minutes.

3 Add coconut milk, stir until well combined and cook for an additional 5-10 minutes. Serve and enjoy.

EGG DROP SOUP

SERVES: 4   TIME: 20 MINUTES

- 3 scoops Bone Broth Protein (Pure) mixed in 36 ounces water (or 4 cups chicken bone broth)
- 2 bunches baby bok choy, thinly sliced
- ½ cup sliced mushrooms
- 1 tablespoon ground ginger
- 1 tablespoon coconut aminos
- 1 teaspoon sea salt
- 1 teaspoon ground white pepper
- 4 large eggs
- 2 egg yolks
- green onions, thinly sliced

1 In a large pot over medium heat, bring bone broth to a very low simmer. Add in bok choy, mushrooms, ginger, coconut aminos, salt and white pepper and simmer for 10–12 minutes.

2 Whisk eggs and egg yolks in a small bowl and, holding a fork over the bowl, gently pour eggs into the pot through the fork tines.

3 Lightly whisk broth and gently stir in green onions.

4 Ladle into bowls and top with more green onions if desired.

AVGOLEMONO

SERVES: 4   TIME: 30 MINUTES

- 3 scoops Bone Broth Protein (Pure) mixed in 36 ounces water (or 4 cups chicken bone broth)
- 2 cups water
- 1 cup brown rice
- 1 teaspoon sea salt
- 2 cups cooked shredded chicken
- 3 eggs
- juice from 2 large lemons

1 In a large pot over medium heat, add bone broth, water, rice and sea salt. Cook for 30 minutes, or until rice is tender. Reduce heat to medium-low and add chicken.

2 In a medium bowl, whisk eggs and lemon juice together until lighter in color.

3 Take 2 cups of liquid from soup, and, stirring constantly, carefully add it in a thin stream to eggs and juice.

4 While stirring soup, add egg mixture to simmering pot and stir until thickened, about 2-3 minutes.

5 Remove from heat and serve.

CREAMY TOMATO SOUP

SERVES: 6–8   TIME: 20 MINUTES

- 3 cloves garlic, pressed or minced
- 1 tablespoon coconut oil
- 2 BPA-free cans (28 ounces each) salt-free diced tomatoes
- 1 can (14 ounces) coconut milk (full-fat)
- ½ teaspoon sea salt
- 2 teaspoons apple cider vinegar
- 4 scoops Bone Broth Protein (Pure) mixed in 36 ounces water (or 4 cups bone broth)
- fresh basil, minced
- fresh cracked pepper

1 In a medium pot over medium-low heat, sauté garlic in oil for 5 minutes, or until lightly browned.

2 Add tomatoes, coconut milk, sea salt, vinegar and bone broth, stirring to combine.

3 Cook until hot. Top each serving with fresh basil and fresh cracked pepper.

BEEF & BUTTERNUT SQUASH SOUP

SERVES: 6   TIME: 35 MINUTES

- 4 scoops Bone Broth Protein (Pure) mixed in 48 ounces water (or 6 cups beef bone broth)
- 1½ teaspoons ground ginger
- 1 teaspoon chipotle pepper
- 1 teaspoon cumin
- ½ teaspoon sea salt
- 1 pound beef, sliced or cubed
- 1 yellow onion, diced
- 1 medium butternut squash, cubed

1 In a large pot over medium heat, bring bone broth, spices and sea salt to a simmer.

2 Add remaining ingredients and return to a simmer. Reduce heat to low and simmer for 25 minutes.

GINGERED BEEF & BROCCOLI SOUP

SERVES: 4   TIME: 25 MINUTES

- 2 teaspoons coconut oil
- ¼ cup coconut aminos
- 2 tablespoons apple cider vinegar
- 2 cloves garlic, smashed and chopped
- ½ teaspoon red pepper flakes
- 1 tablespoon fresh grated ginger root
- 1 pound grass-fed ribeye, sliced into strips
- 1 scoop Bone Broth Protein (Pure) mixed with 12 ounces of water (or 1 ½ cups beef bone broth)
- 1 head of broccoli, broken into pieces
- 1 tablespoon sesame seeds

1 In a crockpot, place coconut oil, coconut aminos, vinegar, garlic, red pepper and ginger.

2 Add meat into crockpot and flip to coat.

3 Pour in bone broth and stir. Cook on low for 6-8 hours.

4 Add broccoli about an hour before serving.

5 Sprinkle sesame seeds over top and serve.

TASTY TURKEY BURGERS

SERVES: 2–4   TIME: 20 MINUTES

- ½ onion, diced
- 1 pound ground turkey
- 1 scoop Bone Broth Protein (Pure or Turmeric)
- 1 teaspoon sea salt
- ½ teaspoon garlic powder
- ½ teaspoon turmeric powder (remove if using Turmeric BBP)
- ¼ teaspoon paprika
- ¼ teaspoon coriander
- ¼ teaspoon black pepper
- romaine lettuce or sprouted grain bun

1 In a medium sauté pan over medium heat, sauté onion until tender, about 8-10 minutes.

2 In a medium bowl, combine onion with turkey, protein powder and seasonings.

3 Form into four patties and grill until internal temp reaches 165 F.

4 Serve on romaine lettuce wrap or sprouted grain bun.

MUSHROOM MISO SOUP

SERVES: 2–4   TIME: 35 MINUTES

- 3 scoops Bone Broth Protein (Pure) mixed in 36 ounces water (or 4 cups chicken bone broth and ½ cup water)
- 1 cup baby portabella mushrooms
- ½ red onion, chopped
- 3 cloves garlic, pressed or minced
- 1 tablespoon fresh grated ginger root
- ¼ cup dried wakame
- 3 tablespoons mellow white or garbanzo miso
- half-bunch scallions, chopped

1 In a medium pot over medium-high heat, bring bone broth to a rolling simmer. Add mushrooms, onion, garlic, ginger and wakame. Reduce heat to medium and simmer for 15 minutes. Reduce heat to medium-low and remove 1½ cups of broth.

2 Whisk broth into miso and add to soup. Hold at low heat for 5 minutes before serving.

3 Top each bowl with scallions.

BROCCOLI CAULIFLOWER SOUP

SERVES: 4   TIME: 30 MINUTES

- 5 scoops Bone Broth Protein (Pure or Turmeric) mixed in 60 ounces water (or 8 cups chicken bone broth)
- 1 tablespoon grated turmeric root (remove if using Turmeric BBP)
- 2 cloves garlic, pressed or minced
- $\frac{1}{2}$ teaspoon sea salt
- 1 head of broccoli, chopped into small pieces
- 1 head of cauliflower, chopped into small pieces
- 1 medium yellow onion, diced
- 1 cup dry, raw cashews, ground into powder
- pepper, to taste

1 In a large pot over medium heat, heat broth, turmeric, garlic and sea salt to a simmer.

2 While simmering, add broccoli, cauliflower and onion. Simmer for 10 minutes.

3 Add ground cashews and pepper and stir for 5 minutes. Remove from heat and stir again before serving.

SLOW COOKER SCALLOPED SWEET POTATOES

SERVES: 6-8   PREP: 15 MINUTES   TIME: 3 HOURS

- 1 tablespoon grass-fed butter
- 1 garlic clove, smashed
- 3 large sweet potatoes, sliced thin
- 1 yellow onion, diced
- ½ teaspoon sea salt
- 1½ tablespoons chili powder
- 1 teaspoon cumin
- 2 cups shredded goat or sheep milk cheese
- 2 eggs
- 1½ cups coconut milk (full-fat)
- 1 scoop Bone Broth Protein (Pure)

1 Butter the inside of the crockpot and rub with smashed garlic clove. Mince garlic clove and set aside.

2 In the bottom of the crockpot, add one layer of sweet potatoes. Top with garlic, onion, sea salt, chili powder, cumin and cheese. Keep layering sweet potatoes, garlic, onion, sea salt, spices and cheese.

3 Whisk eggs, coconut milk and protein powder together and pour over sweet potato mixture.

4 Cover, turn crockpot to high and cook for 2½-3 hours.

"NOODLE" BOWLS

SERVES: 4   TIME: 40 MINUTES

- 3 chicken breasts
- 2 tablespoons olive oil, divided
- 1 tablespoon sea salt
- 1 tablespoon pepper
- ½ medium red onion, diced
- 3 stalks celery, chopped
- 6 carrots, chopped
- 4 cups chopped kale, stems removed
- 5 scoops Bone Broth Protein (Pure) mixed in 60 ounces of water (or 8 cups chicken bone broth)
- 3 medium zucchini, spiralized into noodles
- sea salt and pepper, to taste
- basil or parsley, to taste

1 Preheat the oven to 325 F. Line a baking sheet with parchment paper. Place chicken on the sheet, drizzle with 1 tablespoon olive oil and add sea salt and pepper. Place in oven and bake for 25-30 minutes.

2 In a large stockpot over medium heat, add remainder of olive oil, onion, celery and carrots and cook for 8-10 minutes. Add in kale and broth. Turn heat to low and let simmer for 25 minutes.

3 Take the chicken out of the oven and allow to cool for 5 minutes. Using two forks, shred the chicken and add to the stockpot. Simmer for another 15 minutes.

4 Using a spiralizer, zoodle your zucchini into noodles (each zucchini is enough for two servings).

5 Place a serving of noodles in a soup bowl and scoop out soup to pour over "zoodles." Add salt and pepper to taste.

6 Top with basil or parsley. Serve hot.

CHICKEN SALAD

SERVES: 1–2   TIME: 10 MINUTES

- cooked chicken breast, shredded or cut into small pieces
- 1 celery stalk, chopped
- 6–8 grapes, sliced
- small handful walnuts, chopped
- 1 tablespoon kefir
- 1 teaspoon dijon mustard
- 1 scoop Bone Broth Protein (Pure or Turmeric)
- 1 teaspoon black pepper
- $^{1}/_{2}$ teaspoon sea salt
- fresh spinach or lettuce

1 In a medium bowl, mix chicken, celery, grapes and a small handful of walnuts.

2 Mix in kefir, mustard, protein powder, pepper and salt.

3 Serve on bed of spinach or romaine lettuce.

EGG SALAD

SERVES: 2–4   TIME: 10 MINUTES

- 5 hard-boiled eggs
- ¼ cup celery
- ¼ cup raw pecans
- ½ cup Vegenaise
- ¼ cup raisins
- 1 scoop Bone Broth Protein (Pure or Turmeric)
- sea salt and black pepper

1 Chop eggs, celery and pecans.

2 In a medium bowl, combine all ingredients together.

3 Serve chilled.

TUNA SALAD

SERVES: 2   PREP: 10 MINUTES   TIME: 1 HOUR

- 1 can (5-6 ounces) wild-caught tuna, drained and flaked
- ¼ cup organic mayonnaise
- ½ scoop Bone Broth Protein (Pure or Turmeric)
- 1 rib celery, finely chopped
- 2 tablespoons minced onion
- 1 tablespoon Dijon mustard
- 1-2 tablespoons unsweetened dried cranberries
- fresh lemon juice, to taste
- sea salt and pepper, to taste

1 In a medium bowl, combine tuna, mayonnaise, protein powder, celery, onion, mustard and cranberries.

2 Season with lemon juice, salt and pepper. Mix until well combined.

3 Chill for at least 1 hour before serving.

TUNA SALAD

SNACKS
& BARS

SWEET POTATO HUMMUS

SERVES: 4   PREP: 45 MINUTES   TIME: 2 HOURS

- 1½ pounds sweet potato
- ½ cup tahini
- 1 scoop Bone Broth Protein (Pure)
- 2 large garlic cloves
- ¼ cup lime juice
- 2 tablespoons lemon juice
- 1 teaspoon sea salt
- ½ teaspoon pepper
- olive oil (garnish)
- ¼ cup cilantro (garnish)

1 Chop the sweet potatoes into large chunks and add to a pot of boiling water.

2 Let mixture boil for 30-40 minutes, or until sweet potatoes are soft.

3 Drain the water and sweet potatoes through a sieve and carefully peel the skins off of the sweet potatoes.

4 Add the sweet potatoes to the food processor with tahini, protein powder, garlic, lime juice, lemon juice, sea salt and pepper, and purée until smooth.

5 Refrigerate the hummus in an airtight container until cooled and then garnish with olive oil and chopped cilantro before serving.

ALMOND CACAO BAR

ALMOND CACAO BAR

SERVES: 6-8   PREP: 15 MINUTES   TIME: 2 HOURS

- 1 cup raw almond butter
- $1/2$ cup raw honey
- 1 teaspoon vanilla
- $1/8$ teaspoon sea salt
- 1 cup gluten-free oats
- 4 scoops Bone Broth Protein (Pure)
- $1/2$ cup cacao nibs

1 In a medium bowl, whisk together almond butter, honey, vanilla and sea salt.

2 Add oats, protein powder and cacao nibs and combine. Form into bar or cookie shapes and refrigerate.

BLUEBERRY MACADAMIA BAR

SERVES: 6   PREP: 15 MINUTES   TIME: 2 HOURS

- $1/2$ cup melted coconut butter
- $1/4$ cup raw honey
- 1 teaspoon vanilla extract
- $1/8$ teaspoon sea salt
- 4 scoops Bone Broth Protein (Pure)
- $1/2$ cup dried blueberries
- $1/2$ cup chopped raw macadamia nuts
- 3 tablespoons water

1 In a medium bowl, whisk together butter, honey, vanilla and sea salt. Add protein powder and combine. Add remaining ingredients and combine.

2 Pour into a greased loaf pan. Refrigerate for 1-2 hours and then cut into bar or cookie shapes.

ALMOND FIG BAR

SERVES: 4   PREP: 15 MINUTES   TIME: 4 HOURS

- 1 cup dried figs
- 1 cup raw almond butter
- 1 tablespoon flax meal
- 2 scoops Bone Broth Protein (Pure)
- 2 tablespoons raw honey

1 Line an 8-inch baking pan with parchment paper and set aside.

2 In a food processor, add all ingredients and blend until dough starts to form into a ball.

3 Press the dough evenly into the pan and refrigerate for 3–4 hours, or until the bars set.

4 Cut into squares and store in an airtight container.

GLUTEN-FREE BLUEBERRY MUFFINS

SERVES: 12   PREP: 20 MINUTES   TIME: 45 MINUTES

- 1 cup gluten-free oat flour
- ½ cup almond flour
- 2 scoops Bone Broth Protein (Pure)
- ½ teaspoon baking soda
- ¼ teaspoon sea salt
- 3 eggs
- ½ cup raw honey
- ½ cup applesauce
- 1 teaspoon vanilla extract
- 1 teaspoon apple cider vinegar
- ⅛ cup melted coconut oil
- 1 cup fresh or frozen blueberries

1 Preheat the oven to 350 degrees F. Line a standard muffin tin with liners and set aside.

2 In a large mixing bowl, whisk dry ingredients of oat flour, almond flour, protein powder, baking soda and sea salt.

3 In a separate bowl, add eggs, honey, applesauce, vanilla, vinegar and oil. Stir until well combined.

4 Slowly add in dry mixture to wet mixture and stir well.

5 Fold in blueberries into the batter.

6 Bake for 25-35 minutes, or until golden brown on top.

CARROT CAKE BAR

SERVES: 10–12   TIME: 35 MINUTES

- 1 cup Medjool dates, pitted and halved
- ½ cup coconut oil, melted
- 1 teaspoon vanilla extract
- 2 teaspoons cinnamon
- 2 eggs
- ¼ teaspoon sea salt
- 3 scoops Bone Broth Protein (Pure)
- 1½ cups shredded carrots
- ½ cup raw walnut pieces
- 1½ cups gluten-free oats
- ¾ cup raisins

1 Preheat the oven to 375 degrees F. Line a 9-inch pie pan or 8-inch square dish with parchment paper.

2 In a medium bowl, mix dates, oil, vanilla and cinnamon.

3 In a large bowl, whisk eggs, sea salt and protein powder together until eggs are lighter in color.

4 Add date mixture and whisk to combine. Add remaining ingredients and stir to combine. Bake for 20 minutes, or until done.

PECAN PIE BAR

SERVES: 6   PREP: 15 MINUTES   TIME: 2 HOURS

- 1½ cups raw pecans
- 1 scoop Bone Broth Protein (Pure)
- ¼ teaspoon sea salt
- 2 cups Medjool dates, pitted
- ¼ teaspoon cinnamon

 In a food processor, place pecans and pulse into fine pieces. Add protein powder and sea salt; pulse until combined.

 Add dates and cinnamon, and process until sticky.

3 Form into bar shapes and refrigerate until ready to eat.

APPLE PIE BAR

SERVES: 8–10   PREP: 15 MINUTES   TIME: 2 HOURS

- ½ cup raw walnuts
- ½ cup raw cashews
- 4 scoops Bone Broth Protein (Pure)
- 2 teaspoons apple pie spice
- zest of half a lemon
- ¼ teaspoon sea salt
- 1 cup Medjool dates, pitted and halved
- 1½ cups loosely packed dried apples
- 1 tablespoon coconut oil
- 1 teaspoon vanilla extract

1 In a food processor, place walnuts and cashews and pulse into fine pieces.

2 Add protein powder, spice, lemon zest and sea salt; pulse until combined.

3 Add dates, apples, oil and vanilla, and process until combined and sticky.

4 Form into bar shapes and refrigerate until ready to eat.

DESSERTS

FROZEN CHOCOLATE BANANAS

SERVES: 4   PREP: 15 MINUTES   TIME: 1 HOUR

- 2 bananas, halved
- 4 popsicle sticks or chopsticks
- 1/2 cup coconut oil
- 1/4 cup raw honey
- 1/3 cup cocoa powder
- 1 scoop Bone Broth Protein (Pure, Chocolate or Vanilla)
- 1/2 cup chopped raw walnuts

1 Insert a popsicle stick or chopstick into each banana half. Place on a plate in the freezer.

2 Melt oil and whisk in honey, then cocoa powder and protein powder. Allow to cool to room temperature.

3 Remove bananas from the freezer and drizzle mixture over frozen bananas, covering thoroughly. Then top with chopped walnuts.

4 Return to the freezer until chocolate is fully frozen and ready to enjoy.

RASPBERRY ICE CREAM

SERVES: 4   PREP: 5 MINUTES   TIME: 1 HOUR

- 1 can (14 ounces) coconut milk (full-fat)
- 5 Medjool dates, pitted and halved
- 1 scoop Bone Broth Protein (Pure or Vanilla)
- ½ teaspoon vanilla extract
- 2 ½ cups raspberries
- 2 tablespoons lemon juice
- ¾ teaspoon lemon zest

1 In a high-speed blender, purée coconut milk, dates and protein powder until completely smooth.

2 Add in vanilla, raspberries, lemon juice and lemon zest to the coconut mixture. Purée on high until well blended.

3 Pour mixture into a glass container and store in the freezer for an hour. Then add into an ice cream machine and use according to the manufacturer's instructions.

4 In a large glass container with a lid, add ice cream and place in the freezer for at least one hour or overnight.

NO-BAKE
CHOCOLATE
CHIP COOKIES

NO-BAKE CHOCOLATE CHIP COOKIES

SERVES: 6   PREP: 10 MINUTES   TIME: 2 HOURS

- 1½ cups raw almond butter
- ¼ cup raw honey
- 1 teaspoon vanilla extract
- ¼ teaspoon sea salt
- 1 scoop Bone Broth Protein (Pure)
- ½ cup dark chocolate chips

1 In a medium bowl, stir almond butter, honey, vanilla and salt together. Add protein powder and combine thoroughly.

2 Stir in chocolate chips and refrigerate. Form into cookie shapes and enjoy.

BANANA CHIA PUDDING

SERVES: 3–4   PREP: 10 MINUTES   TIME: 20 MINUTES

- 1 cup coconut milk (full-fat)
- ¼ cup ground chia seeds
- 5 tablespoons raw honey
- 1 banana
- 1 teaspoon vanilla extract
- 1 scoop Bone Broth Protein (Pure)
- ¼ teaspoon pumpkin spice or cinnamon

1 In a food processor or blender, place all ingredients and blend for 1 minute.

2 Refrigerate for 10–15 minutes before serving.

CASHEW COOKIES

SERVES: 6   PREP: 15 MINUTES   TIME: 1 HOUR

- 1¼ cups raw cashews
- 1 scoop Bone Broth Protein (Pure)
- ¼ teaspoon sea salt
- 1 cup Medjool dates, pitted and halved
- 1 tablespoon raw honey
- 1 tablespoon coconut oil, melted

 In a food processor, place cashews and pulse into fine pieces. Add protein powder and sea salt; pulse until combined.

 Add dates, honey and oil; process until combined and sticky.

3 Form into ball and refrigerate until ready to eat.

KEY LIME PIE

SERVES: 6-8   PREP: 15 MINUTES   TIME: 2 HOURS

Crust:
- 3 cups raw walnuts
- 2 cups Medjool dates, pitted
- 1 teaspoon vanilla extract
- dash of sea salt

Filling:
- 1¼ cup raw cashews (soaked overnight)
- 1 scoop Bone Broth Protein (Pure)
- zest of 2 limes
- ¼ teaspoon sea salt
- 1 cup Medjool dates, pitted
- 1 tablespoon raw honey
- 1 tablespoon melted coconut oil
- 2 tablespoons lime juice

1 In a food processor, blend together the walnuts, dates, vanilla and sea salt until dough is formed.

2 Spread dough evenly in the bottom of an ungreased 9-inch springform pan. Place the pan in the freezer for 30 minutes.

3 In a blender on low speed, blend all filling ingredients until well combined.

4 Remove crust from the freezer. Pour filling mixture on top of crust, cover the pan and replace cake in the freezer.

5 Freeze for at least 2 hours. Defrost cake in the refrigerator for 20 minutes before serving.

RASPBERRY SMOOTHIE

SERVES: 2   TIME: 5 MINUTES

- 1 cup coconut milk yogurt
- 1 banana
- $\frac{1}{2}$ cup frozen raspberries
- $\frac{1}{4}$ cup nut milk
- 1 scoop Bone Broth Protein (Pure or Vanilla)
- $\frac{1}{4}$ cup desiccated coconut flakes
- 1 teaspoon chia seeds
- 1 teaspoon hemp seeds
- 2 tablespoons raw almond butter
- 1 teaspoon ground flax (optional)

1 In a high-speed blender, place all ingredients and purée until smooth.

CHOCOLATE MILK SHAKE

- ¼ cup raw cashews (soaked overnight)
- 1 cup frozen banana
- 2 tablespoons cocoa powder
- 12 ounces nut milk
- 1 tablespoon raw honey
- 1 scoop Bone Broth Protein (Pure or Chocolate)
- vanilla extract, to taste

1 In a high-speed blender, place all ingredients and purée until smooth, adding water and ice to blend as necessary.

INDEX

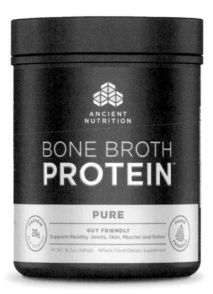

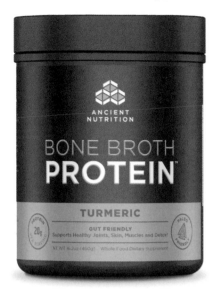

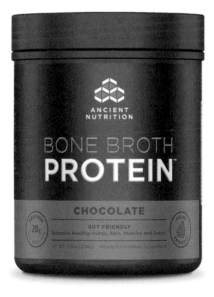

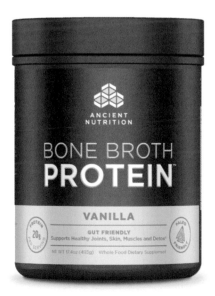